Spotlight on Reading

Inferring

Grades 1–2

Carson-Dellosa Publishing, LLC
Greensboro, North Carolina

Credits

Layout and Cover Design: Van Harris

Development House: The Research Masters

Cover Photo: © Digital Vision

Visit *carsondellosa.com* for correlations to Common Core, state, national, and Canadian provincial standards.

Carson-Dellosa Publishing, LLC
PO Box 35665
Greensboro, NC 27425 USA
www.carsondellosa.com

ISBN 978-1-60996-489-4
10-207217784

About the Book

The activities in *Inferring* are designed to improve students' reading comprehension. The skill of inferring—using information to draw logical conclusions—is a higher-level thinking skill, and a difficult one for young students to master. Early readers need to practice the application of this skill over and over again in a variety of ways.

Inferring requires the reader to make educated guesses based on prior knowledge and on information that is implied, but not directly stated. The lessons in this book have a variety of activities to make learning the skill of inferring fun. The exercises increase in difficulty as the book progresses, so students practice more advanced skills as they work through the pages.

The variety of activities and formats in this book provide an opportunity for teachers to supplement regular lessons with reinforcement and independent practice. Have students work with partners or teams to complete the more challenging activities.

● ●

Table of Contents

Summer Fun

Look at the pictures on the bottom of the page and cut out the pictures of things that belong at the beach. Paste them into the big picture.

Try this: Draw a picture of a toy you use at the beach in the empty box. Cut it out. Paste it in the picture too.

Name _____

Circle the things in the picture that do not belong in the park. Then answer the questions below the picture.

Name one thing that does not belong. _____

_____

How do you know it does not belong on the playground? _____

_____

Ready for School

Look at the pictures below. Circle the items that belong at school. Draw a line to match each item to the correct student.

A

B

C

D

E

F

RED   BLUE   YELLO

G

H

I

J

Try this: On another sheet of paper, draw a picture of where you would use the items not circled on this page.

In the City

What do people do in the city? Cut out the small pictures below. Paste them where they belong in the big picture of the city. Answer the question below.

1. How did you know where to paste the pictures? _____

_____

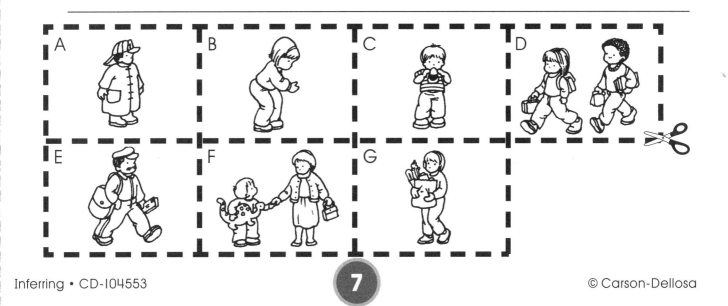

7

In the Country

Look at the picture. Circle the things that do not belong on a farm. Look at the animal pictures. Color the farm animals below the big picture. Answer the questions below.

Name the animal that is not colored. _____

Where does it belong? _____ How do you know? _____

_____

Can You Fix This Story?

These pictures are all mixed up. Can you figure out what order they go in? Cut the pictures out. Paste them on another piece of paper in the right order so they tell a story.

He rode his bike to the park.

He put his new bike away.

He rode back home.

Wow! Thanks!

Leon got a new bike.

Try this: After you paste the pictures in the right order, write a title for the story. Write a sentence about what you think will happen next.

Name _____

Which Toy Do You Want?

Draw a line to match each child to the correct toy. Answer the questions below.

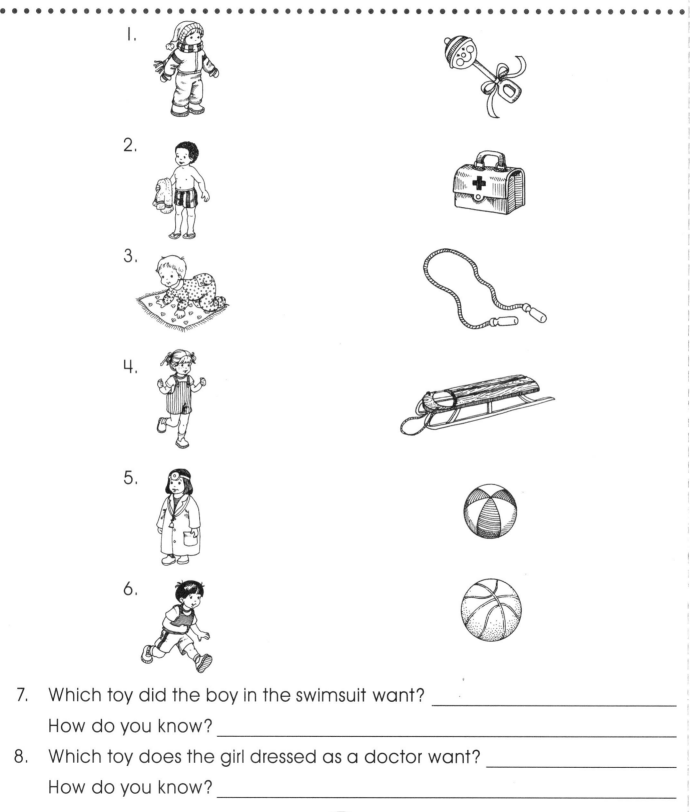

1.

2.

3.

4.

5.

6.

7. Which toy did the boy in the swimsuit want? _____

How do you know? _____

8. Which toy does the girl dressed as a doctor want? _____

How do you know? _____

Inferring • CD-104553

What Is Happening?

Look at the pictures in each row. Circle the picture on the right that shows what happens next.

. . . .

Circle the picture above that gives you clues about what the boy is making.

Circle the picture above that gives you clues about which animal the girl is feeding.

Circle the picture above that gives you clues about which plant will grow.

Which Comes First?

These pictures are out of order. Write **1** in front of the picture that comes first. Write **2** in front of the picture that comes next. Write **3** in front of the picture that comes last. Answer the question below.

• •

_____

_____

_____

How did you know the order of the pictures? _____

_____

What Comes Next?

Look at the pictures in each row. Draw a picture that shows what happens next.

Which clues tell you what happens next? _____

_____

_____

Which clues tell you what happens next? _____

_____

_____

Name _____

The Snowman

Read the sentences. Put a I in front of the sentence that comes first. Number the rest of the sentences in the order they should happen.

· ·

_____ The snowman melted away.

_____ Dark clouds covered the blue sky.

_____ The warm sun came out.

_____ We built a snowman.

_____ Our lawn had a new coat of white snow.

_____ Big, fat flakes of snow came down.

Inferring • CD-104553

Name _____

The Missing Word

Read each sentence. Look at the picture beside each sentence. Use the picture to help you infer which word fills in the blank.

Word Bank

chickens	bat	clown	nap	coat

1. The boy's baseball _____ is under his chair.

2. The _____ in the barn just laid eggs.

3. I put on my new _____ .

4. The funny _____ had a big red nose.

5. The baby needs to take a _____ .

Try this: On another sheet of paper, draw a picture of your favorite food. Write a sentence about the food, but leave one word blank. Give it to a friend. Can your friend use your picture clue to fill in the blank?

Where Am I?

Read the sentences below. Use clues in the sentences to infer where each person is.

• •

1. Stacie rode the merry-go-round. She flew high on the swings. She rode down the slide.
    Where is Stacie? _____

2. Tina walked in the door and hung up her coat. She sat down at her desk, got out her book, and read. Her teacher told her to put the book away. It was time for the spelling test.
    Where is Tina? _____

3. Keisha ran to the barn to see the cows, sheep, chickens, and pony. She was always glad to visit Grandma and Grandpa. She loved to run in the fields, gather the eggs, and ride on the tractor.
    Where do Keisha's grandparents live? _____

    _____

4. Tony followed Mom through the big door. He saw men's shirts and shoes. They walked past the pants and socks. Tony saw racks of dresses. They went to the second floor and found clothes for kids.
    Where are Tony and his mom? _____

    _____

Name_____

What Am I?

Karen was planning a guessing game for her friends. Read the clues and draw a line to match the pictures to the clues.

1. I am round and orange.
   You might give me a grin.
   I make a great pie.

2. Do not slip on my peel!
   I am green before I am ripe.
   I am yellow when I am good to eat.

3. I am the color of snow.
   I keep my fur very clean.
   I drink milk and catch mice.

4. I have a nose. I have a tail.
   If you ride on my back,
   we will gallop along the trail.

5. I keep the sun out of your eyes.
   You might wear me as you
   round up a herd of cattle.

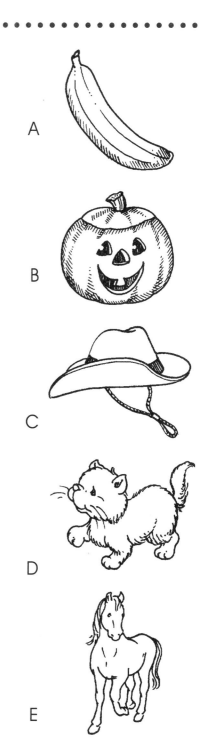

A

B

C

D

E

Name _____

Where Would You Go?

Look at each shopper's list. Look at the stores. Where should each person shop? Match each list to a store. Write the matching store's number on the line.

• •

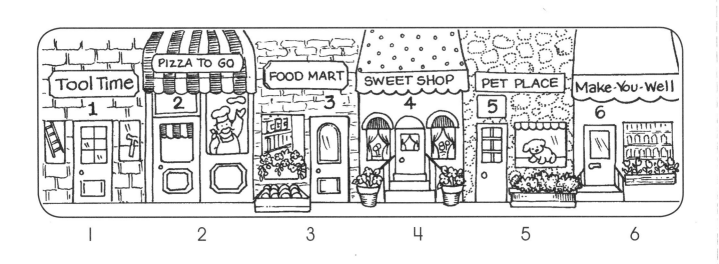

A. John needs:

   eggs
   milk
   bread   _____

B. Susie needs:

   kitty litter
   dog food
   hamster cage   _____

C. Juanita needs:

   cold pills
   cough drops
   thermometer   _____

D. Jose needs:

   gumdrops
   lollipops
   candy bars   _____

E. Steve needs:

   nails
   saw
   hammer   _____

F. Karen needs:

   pizza
   soda
   salad   _____

Inferring • CD-104553

Name _____

Read each of the stories. Use clues in the stories to infer which food each person likes.

● ●

1. Mom called Emory a rabbit when he asked for his favorite orange vegetable.
   What vegetable does Emory want? _____

2. Hestor likes to pick the fruit from trees in his orchard. The round, ripe fruit has a red skin.
   What did Hestor pick to eat? _____

3. Myong helps Grandpa dig up her favorite vegetable. She loves to eat this baked vegetable with butter.
   What did Myong help Grandpa dig up? _____

4. Frederico loves this fuzzy, juicy fruit. Mom peels them to make his favorite pie.
   What fruit does Frederico like best? _____

5. Tony picked six ears of his favorite vegetable. Tony will butter one before he eats it right off the cob.
   What did Tony pick? _____

Try this: What is your favorite fruit? Write two sentences that tell about it, but do not write its name. Show the sentences to a friend. Can your friend guess your favorite fruit?

Who Needs to Sneeze?

Look at the animals. They all have colds. Circle **Yes** or **No** for each of the following sentences.

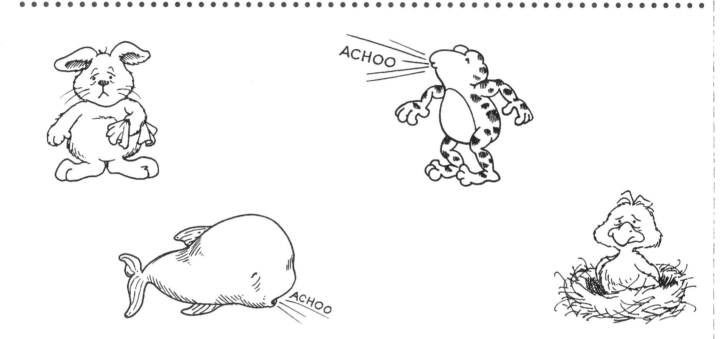

1. A bird with a cold would go to a nest to take a nap.   Yes   No

2. A whale who sneezed could make big waves in the water.   Yes   No

3. Both the bird and the whale could use leaves as handkerchiefs.   Yes   No

4. A rabbit can climb a tree to sleep when he is ill.   Yes   No

5. A frog that coughed could shake up the ocean.   Yes   No

6. A whale with a cold could crawl onto a lily pad to rest.   Yes   No

20

Name _____

Read the stories. Infer the answers to the questions.

• •

Sue Lee rode to the store. She rode up a big hill. She had to pump hard. It was easy to coast down the other side. Sue Lee went very fast. She had to use her brakes.

1. What did Sue Lee ride to the store?

a horse   a skateboard   a bike

What clues helped you infer the answer? _____

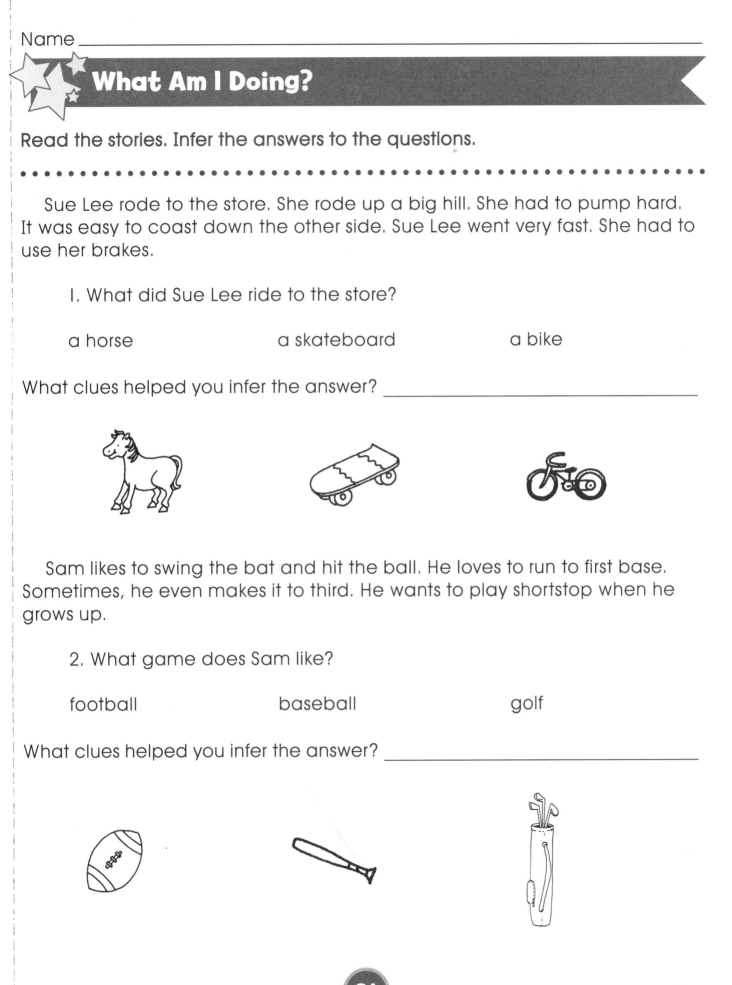

Sam likes to swing the bat and hit the ball. He loves to run to first base. Sometimes, he even makes it to third. He wants to play shortstop when he grows up.

2. What game does Sam like?

football   baseball   golf

What clues helped you infer the answer? _____

Name _____

What Will David Do?

Read the story. Use clues in the sentences to infer the answers to the questions below.

• •

David has to move. His dad has a new job in the city. David has to pack all his toys. He will give the old ones away. He will put the new ones in a big box. He will have to say goodbye to his friends. David will not be able to play in the barn anymore. This makes him sad.

1. Do you think David lives in the city right now? _____ Why or why not?

_____

_____

2. What do you think David will do with the new toys? _____

_____

Why? _____

_____

3. Do you think David will miss his friends? _____ Why or why not?

_____

_____

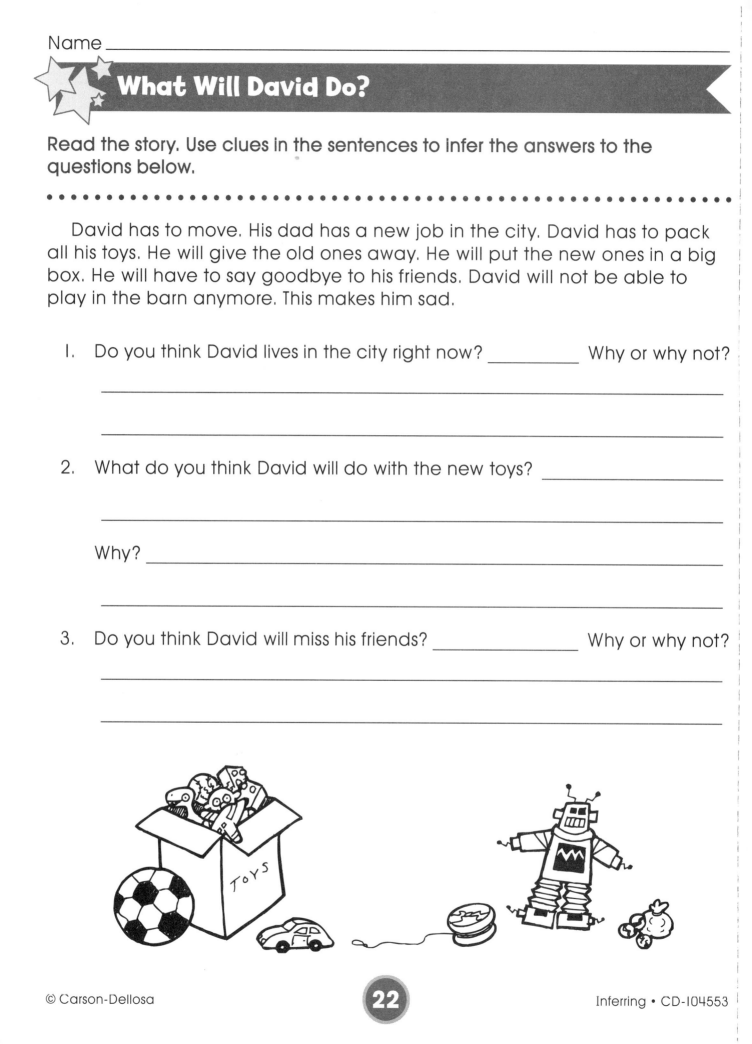

Time to Get Up!

The girl is asleep in the picture on the bottom right. Cut out the pictures and paste them on another piece of paper in the right order. Answer question below.

How did you know the right order of the pictures? _____

_____

Name _____

As Days Grow Short

Read the story. Think about clues in the sentences. Use the clues to infer the answers to the questions below.

• •

Joe saw an animal with a gray tail climb down from a tree branch. It raced across the ground and picked up an acorn. It ran back to the tree and hid the acorn in a hole in the tree trunk. Joe knew the animal was storing food to eat during the winter.

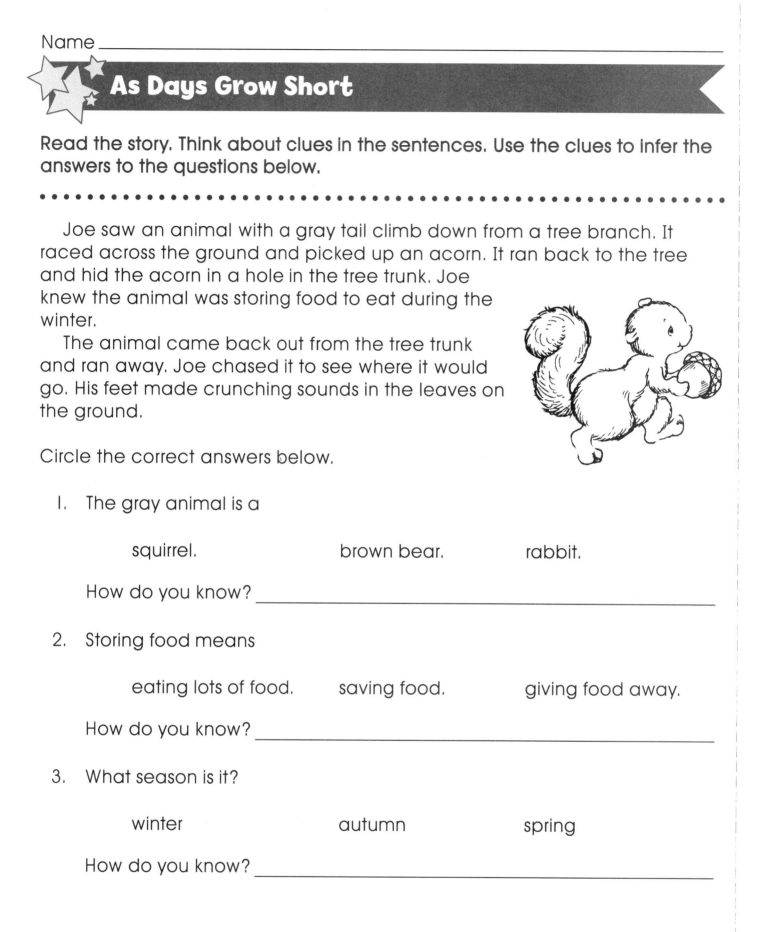

The animal came back out from the tree trunk and ran away. Joe chased it to see where it would go. His feet made crunching sounds in the leaves on the ground.

Circle the correct answers below.

1. The gray animal is a

    squirrel.   brown bear.   rabbit.

    How do you know? _____

2. Storing food means

    eating lots of food.   saving food.   giving food away.

    How do you know? _____

3. What season is it?

    winter   autumn   spring

    How do you know? _____

24   Inferring • CD-104553

Name _____

Read the story. Use clues in the story to infer the answers to the questions below.

• •

Toby was ready to go for his morning walk. He peeked outside and looked around the yard.

"Where is Sam?" Toby asked. He wanted to take a nice, quiet walk by himself. He did not want that pesky Sam following him. He could not see Sam anywhere.

Toby walked slowly across the grass. He looked for bright red flowers. They were his favorite food.

Someone made a noise nearby. "Sniff, sniff." The sound got louder and louder.

Oh, no! Toby thought. *It is Sam. He is coming this way.* Toby stood very still.

Sam found him anyway. Sam sniffed Toby's feet. Sam licked Toby's nose. Toby did not like that. Toby pulled his feet and head into his shell. Sam barked at him. Toby was happy that he was safe inside his take-along home.

Draw a picture of Toby	Draw a picture of Sam

1. Circle the clues that tell you what animal Toby is.

Toby pulled his head
and feet into his shell.
Toby listened.
Toby looked for bright
red flowers.

2. Circle the clues that tell you what animal Sam is.

Sam sniffed.
Sam barked.
Sam found Toby.

A Trip to the Farm

Read each story. Read the three endings. Use clues in the story to infer which ending makes sense. Circle the correct answers below.

• •

1. Jade's class was going on a trip. They were going to the farm. A big bus came to get them.

    a. They all went home

    b. They got on the bus.

    c. They went out to play.

2. They rode for a long time. The bus came to a stop. They were at the farm!

    a. They all got off.

    b. They went to the store.

    c. They got on top of the bus.

3. They explored the farm. They went to see the horse. He had a long mane. Jade gave him a carrot.

    a. He ate the carrot.

    b. He neighed.

    c. He galloped away.

Inferring • CD-104553

Playground Fun

Read the list of playground games. Read each story. Choose the game that best fits each story. Write the letter of the game on the blank line.

- -

> A. the swing set   B. the slide   C. the sandbox
>
> D. the seesaw   E. hide-and-go-seek

1. Ella climbed the ladder. She stood on the top step and looked down at the playground. Ella sat and gave herself a push. Ella was playing on_____

   _____

2. Aiden took toys out of his backpack. He handed a dump truck to his little brother. Aiden chose a shovel. He wanted to build a road and a castle. Aiden and his brother were playing in _____

3. Mia and Lucy wanted to play. They both sat. "Hold on tight," Mia said. Mia pushed her feet against the ground. Lucy laughed as she sank. Mia lifted toward the sky. Mia and Lucy were playing on _____

   _____

4. Connor closed his eyes. He began to count to twenty. He heard the foot-steps of his friends as they scattered. Connor knew he would find them. "Ready or not, here I come," shouted Connor. Connor was playing_____

   _____

5. Maya loves to go high. She pulled on the chains and kicked out with her legs. She felt like she was flying. Maya was playing on _____

   _____

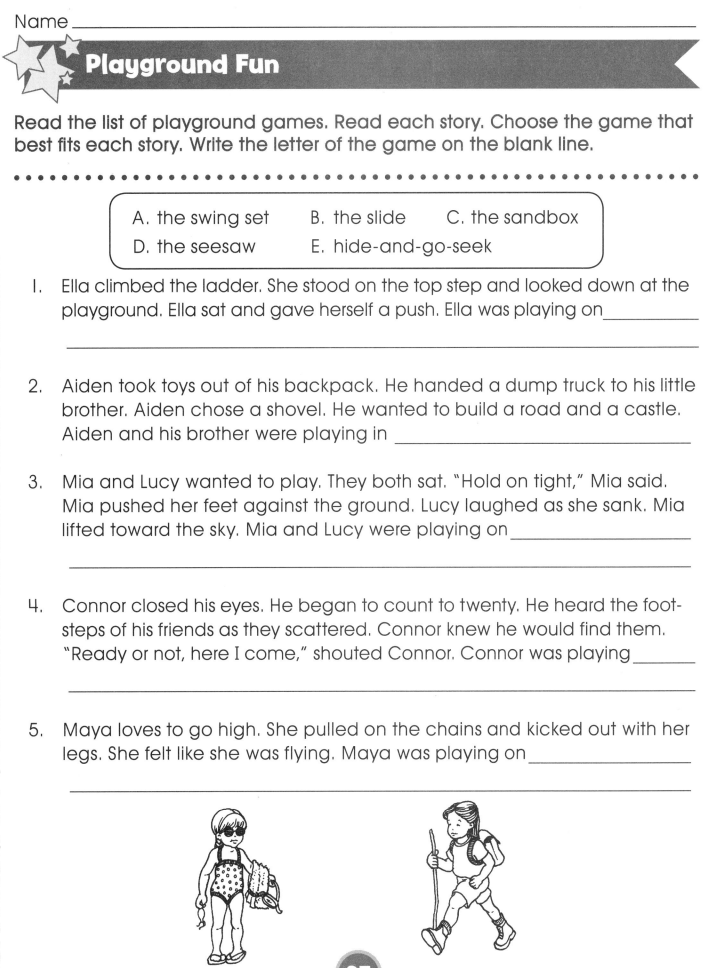

27

Name _____

Pets on Parade

Read all of the riddles. Can you guess what pet each child has? Use the Word Bank to complete each sentence below.

• •

Word Bank				
lizard	spider	fish	bird	snake

Joan said, "My pet is named Polly. She has green, orange, and yellow feathers. She has a sharp beak and she can fly."

"My pet is named Goldie," Billy said. "She has big eyes and fins. She lives in a tank. I cannot hold her, but I love to look at her."

Marla said, "My pet has eight legs. I call him Fuzzy because he has a furry body and furry legs. Some people think my pet can poison you with a bite, but he cannot!"

"My pet is Lizzy," Rob said. "She loves to eat insects. She's a reptile. If you pull on her tail, it might fall off. Do not worry! If it does, she will grow a new one."

Nell said, "I have a pet named Slider. Slider has no legs, just a long, skinny body. His tongue flicks in and out. He swallows his food whole."

1. Polly is a _____

2. Goldie is a _____

3. Fuzzy is a _____

4. Lizzy is a _____

5. Slider is a _____

Inferring • CD-104553

Name _____

Cookie Jar

Read the story. Use the clues in the story to answer the questions below. Circle or write the correct answers.

• •

"Holly, why did you eat so many cookies?" Heather asked.

"I did not eat any cookies," Holly said. "You must have eaten them all!"

"I did not." Heather said.

Each girl was sure the other had eaten most of the cookies. They were angry at each other. They stopped talking and playing together.

Later, when Heather walked across the dining room, she almost stepped on a cookie. "What is this doing here?" she asked. She walked down the hall and knocked on Holly's door.

"Holly! Look what I found on the floor."

"On the floor? How did it get there?" Holly asked.

"I don't know," Heather said, "but we will find out."

The girls got four more cookies from the jar and set them out on a plate. They hid in the closet.

Ed trotted in. He jumped up on a chair, put both front paws on the table, and picked up a cookie. He jumped down and padded out the door with his treat.

Heather and Holly laughed, "Now we know who took the cookies."

1. Who are Holly and Heather?

        friends   brothers   sisters

    What clues told you who they are? _____

    _____

2. How do they feel at the beginning of the story? _____

3. How do they feel at the end of the story? _____

4. Who is Ed?

        a little brother   a dog   a bird

5. What clues told you who Ed is? _____

    _____

Name _____

Read the story. Circle, write, or draw the answers to the questions below.

• •

Lizzie and I decided to hunt bugs. I got a jar and I punched some holes in the lid. Lizzie and I went out to the backyard.

"Where should we look?" I asked. Lizzie's tongue flicked out. It looked like she was pointing to bushes near the porch. Lizzie perched on my shoulder. We got down and crawled under the bushes.

It was dark and damp. We sat very quietly, watching for bugs. I found two ants. I dropped them into the jar.

"You guard the jar, Lizzie. I'll get more bugs." I found a caterpillar and put it in the jar. Then I saw a small, gray spider. It scurried away. I crawled after it, but the spider got away.

I checked the other bugs we'd caught, but they had all disappeared!

Complete the following.

1. Lizzie is a . . .

    cat.   bird.   lizard.

2. Draw a picture of Lizzie.

3. How do you think the child felt when all the bugs disappeared? Why?

    _____

    _____

    _____

Alisha Jones, Private Eye

Read the story below. Use clues in the story to infer the answers to questions on the next page.

• •

Alisha hung a sign outside her clubhouse door. It said:

Alisha Jones, Private Eye

Noah, her neighbor, rode down the driveway. He was on his tricycle. He looked at the sign for a long time. He looked around the yard.

"Where is the yard sale?" he asked.

"There is no yard sale," Alisha said.

"But you have a sign up," Noah said.

Alisha said, "That sign says I am a detective. I solve crimes and I find things that are lost."

"If I lost something, could you find it?" Noah asked.

"I could try," Alisha said.

Noah took Alisha to his house. They went to his room.

Alisha looked around. There were toys everywhere! She was not surprised Noah had lost something. She was surprised he ever found anything.

Noah went over to his closet. He took out a plastic car. It had a slot in the top.

"This is my bank," he said. "Every week I get ten dimes for my allowance. I spend five of them at the mall. I put the other five in here. On Monday, I had a lot of dimes. Now they are all gone! Can you find them for me?"

"First, we need some clues," Alisha said. She shook the bank. She did not hear any dimes. She opened the little door on the bottom of the bank. Two pieces of paper fell out. One was white and one was green. When she read what was written on the white paper, she tried not to laugh. It said:

Dear Noah,

I needed some change for the wash. You had $4.70 in dimes. Here is $5.00.

Thank you.
Love,
Mom

Be a Private Eye

1. How old do you think Noah is? _____

   How can you tell? _____

   _____

2. Why do most people put up homemade signs on Alisha's street?

   _____

   How can you tell?

   _____

3. Was Noah's room messy or neat?

   _____

   How can you tell?

   _____

4. What was the green piece of paper in Noah's bank?

   _____

So They Say

Read each story. Circle the choice that means the same as the **words in bold print.**

• •

1. Jake always did his work late. He wanted to start doing his work on time. Jake wanted to **turn over a new leaf.**

    a. Jake wanted to bring a leaf to school.

    b. Jake wanted to do his work on time.

    c. Jake wanted to turn over his paper.

2. Ann was mad. Her face was red. She yelled at everyone. **She got up on the wrong side of the bed.**

    a. Ann always sleeps on the same side of the bed.

    b. Ann is always mad.

    c. Ann was in a bad mood.

33

Bath Time

Read the story. Use clues in the story to answer the questions below.

• •

Tyler got the shampoo. Holly found a towel. Tyler pulled the tub into the yard. Holly filled it with water.

"Here, Dusty," Holly called.

Dusty raced across the yard. When he saw the tub, his tail drooped. Dusty lay down and rolled over.

"Help me, Tyler," Holly said.

The kids carried Dusty to the tub. Tyler shampooed Dusty while Holly held him.

"Time to rinse off the soap," Tyler said. Just then, Dusty shook. Soap suds flew everywhere. Holly and Tyler were now covered with soap too.

1. Tyler and Holly gave Dusty a

    towel.   tub.   bath.

2. Dusty is a . . .

    cat.   dog.   brother.

3. How do you know what Dusty is?

    _____

4. What do Tyler and Holly need to do when they finish?

    _____

5. Why do you think Dusty lay down when he saw the tub of water?

    _____

Where is Juan?

Read the story. Answer the questions below.

• •

"I'm back," Mom called as she came in the back door. She set two bags on the kitchen table. Isabella put down her book and went to see if she could help Mom. Isabella put cans of soup, beans, and corn away. Mom put milk and eggs in the refrigerator.

"Where is Juan?" Mom asked.

"I don't know," Isabella said. "I will check his room."

Juan was not there. Isabella looked carefully around the room. Juan's glove, bat, and team cap were gone. Isabella ran to the garage. Juan's bike was gone, too. She went back into the kitchen.

"Juan's not here, Mom. I think I know where he is." She looked at the calendar. Now she was sure. "Juan's at baseball practice."

1. Where had Mom been? _____

2. How do you know? _____

3. Who is Juan? _____

4. How do you know? _____

5. How did Isabella know Juan was at baseball practice? _____

    _____

6. Why do you think Isabella looked at the calendar? _____

    _____

Name_____

Read about Marsha and Tim. Circle the correct answers to the questions.

• •

Marsha and Tim want to plant gardens. They went to a store to buy seeds.

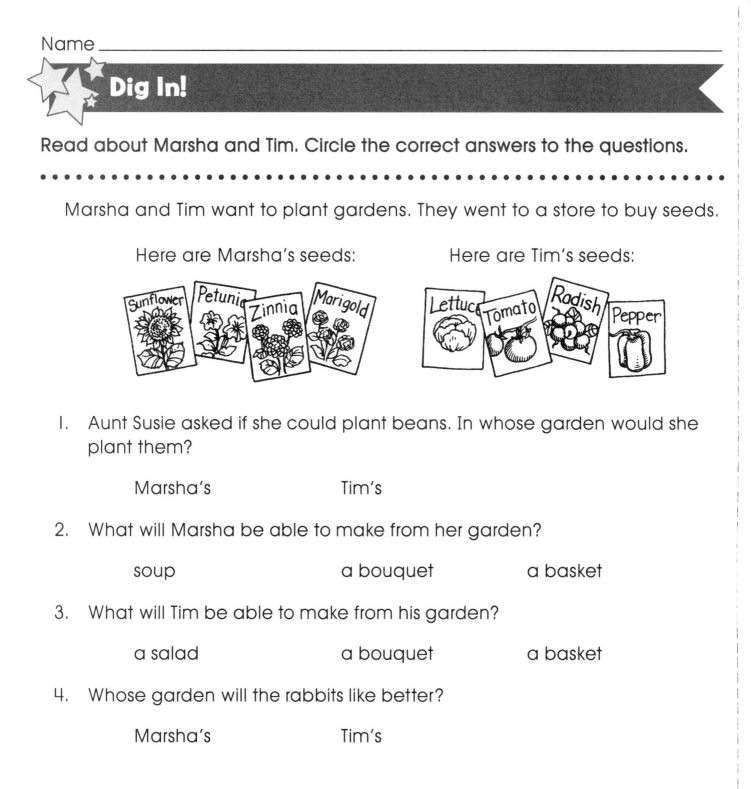

Here are Marsha's seeds: Here are Tim's seeds:

1. Aunt Susie asked if she could plant beans. In whose garden would she plant them?

    Marsha's   Tim's

2. What will Marsha be able to make from her garden?

    soup   a bouquet   a basket

3. What will Tim be able to make from his garden?

    a salad   a bouquet   a basket

4. Whose garden will the rabbits like better?

    Marsha's   Tim's

5. Circle the tools that Marsha and Tim will need.

    A   B   C   D   E

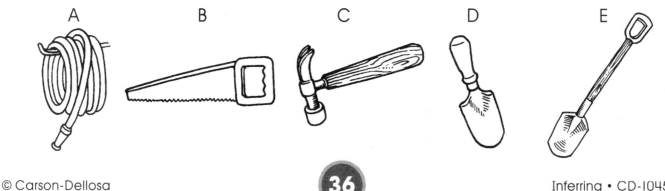

⭐ Special Day

Read the story. Use clues in the story to answer the questions below. Circle the correct answers.

• •

Tyler jumped out of bed and shouted, "Today is the day my friends are coming over for a special play date. My mother said I could invite five friends but I was hoping I could ask eight friends.

He sat down. "Where's Sparky?" Sparky always sat right beside him.

"Wasn't she in your room?" Cindy asked.

"I haven't seen her," said Mom.

"Oh, no," Tyler said. "What if something happened to Sparky?

"Why don't you call her?" asked Dad.

"Sparky. Here, Sparky!" Tyler called.

Sparky did not come, but Tyler heard a scratch at the door. When he opened the door, there was Sparky. She had a balloon tied to her collar. Just then Tyler saw two of his friends he didn't expect. Sparky barked and Tyler was very excited.

1. How did Tyler feel when he woke up?

   excited   worried   lonely

2. How did he feel when no one knew where Sparky was?

   happy   lonely   worried

3. What kind of day is Tyler probably going to have?

   good day   bad day

Name_____

Read the story. Use clues in the story to answer the questions below.

• •

Joan was going to Nell's house for the first time. She carefully read the directions: Walk three blocks from school. On the corner is a large church and a house with yellow shutters. Go around the corner and look for my house. It is green and has a big green tree in the front yard. The house number is 453.

Joan frowned. She looked up and down the street in front of the school. She did not know which way to go!

> Walk three blocks from school. On the corner is a large church and a house with yellow shutters. Go around the corner and look for my house. It is green and has a big tree in the front yard. The house number is 453.

1. What did Nell forget to tell Joan?_____

    _____

    Joan decided to walk west along the street. She walked three blocks. There was a white house with a green roof, an empty lot, and a trailer on the corner.

2. Was Joan at the right corner? _____
    How do you know? _____

    _____

    Joan walked back to her school and tried the other direction. After walking two blocks, she came to a corner with a large church and a house with yellow shutters.

3. What should Joan do now? _____
    Joan turned the corner and began looking for a green house with a big tree in front. There were two green houses with trees. Joan stopped at the first one, then walked up and knocked on Nell's front door.

4. How did Joan know this was Nell's house? _____

    _____

Homework Trouble

Read the story. Use the clues in the story to answer the questions below.

• •

Brad sat at his desk to do his homework. He added up some numbers. While Brad worked, Sammy stretched his paw through the wire cage and tugged at Brad's paper.

"No, Sammy," Brad said. "This is my homework. You can't play with it." Instead he gave Sammy a tissue. Sammy squeaked as he pulled the tissue into his cage. He shredded it and made a new nest.

Brad took a break to play with Sammy. He rubbed Sammy's white fur and tickled his fluffy tail. Brad loved Sammy's long ears.

When Brad finished his homework, he left his paper on the desk and went to watch his favorite TV show. At bedtime, he decided to put his paper and book in his backpack.

His paper was gone, except for one tiny scrap. "Oh, no!" Brad said.

1. What kind of pet is Sammy?_____
   How do you know? _____

2. What kind of homework was Brad doing? _____
   How do you know? _____

3. What happened to Brad's homework? _____
   How do you know? _____

4. How do you think Brad felt? _____

   _____

Letter to Grandma

Read the letter. Use clues in the letter to answer the questions below.

• •

Dear Grandma,

When I woke up this morning at nine o'clock, I thought I had missed the bus. Then I looked outside. Guess what happened while I was sleeping? It was all white outside!

After breakfast, I put on the boots you gave me. I also put on mittens, a hat, and a jacket. I went outside.

I made tracks in the yard. I looked at the hill by our house and I got a great idea. I ran to the garage. I got my favorite toy. Soon I was coasting down the hill. What a day!

Love,
Jake

1. What happened while Jake was sleeping? _____
   _____

2. Why was Jake not late for school? _____
   _____

3. What did Jake get out of the garage? _____
   _____

4. How do you think Jake felt about his day? _____
   _____

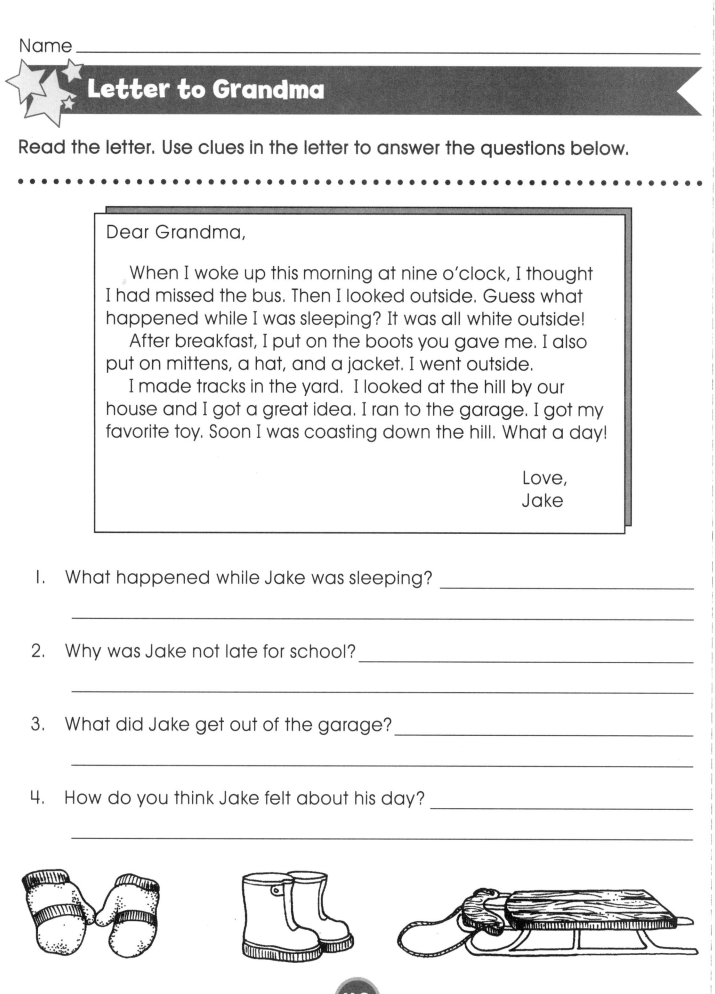

Be a Detective

Read each story. Use clues in the story to infer the meanings of the bold words.

• •

1. It was a **pleasant** day. The sky was blue and the sun was warm. We put on our suits and ran down to the beach.

    dull   nice   sad

2. It was hot outside. Toby went to gather some eggs. All of the hens were asleep **beneath** the porch, where it was shady.

    under   above   on

3. Irma fell down in the yard at lunch. She hurt her arm. The **ache** got worse when she carried a big box for Mrs. Wilson.

    dream   page   pain

4. Some dinosaurs were small, but brachiosaurs were **huge.**

    fast   big   old

5. We would not let a little rain **spoil** our trip to the park. We took our rain-coats and umbrellas.

    ruin   fix   share

> **Try this:** Write a paragraph on a separate piece of paper that uses the word *reading.* The paragraph should have clues that show what the word means.

⭐ Way Out West

Read about Nancy's summer vacation. Use the clues to infer the answers to the questions below.

• •

Nancy spent her summer vacation with Aunt Sara on the Big Pony Ranch in Arizona. The way people on the ranch talked amazed Nancy. Look at the **bold words** in the following sentences. Tell what the words mean by completing each sentence.

1. The **sky-tickling** cactus was as tall as a two-story house.
   Sky-tickling means _____

2. My brother got very angry when he had to put his horse in the barn for the night. He screamed and cried. Everyone laughed when Slim said that my brother knew how to have a **Texas-sized tantrum.**

   Texas-sized tantrum means _____

3. When Ted disappeared from the corral one morning, I could not go riding. I felt very sad. Slim tried to cheer me up because I felt as **low as a snake's belly.**

   As low as a snake's belly means _____

Inferring • CD-104553

Off to the Races

Read the story. Use clues in the story to infer the answers to the questions on the next page.

• •

Herbert was tired of being slow. Harriet always made fun of him because she was fast and he was not. She called him pokey. All of his friends called him pokey too.

Herbert decided to practice running so he could learn to be fast. He drew a line in the dirt with his toes. He stood behind the line and said, "Ready. Set. Go!" Every day, Herbert ran as fast as he could.

"This would be a lot easier if I didn't have to carry this shell on my back," Herbert always said. But he did not quit. He kept practicing.

The next time Herbert saw Harriet, she made fun of him again. "Herbert, all you do is crawl along," she said.

Herbert was ready. "I challenge you to a race," he said.

Harriet hopped up and down and laughed.

"It won't be a race," she said. "I will win, paws down."

"We'll see about that," Herbert said.

The next morning, with all their friends gathered for the race, Herbert and Harriet lined up side by side. Harriet was still laughing. Herbert clamped his jaws together and looked down the trail.

"Ready. Set. Go!" the crowd shouted.

Herbert pushed off with his four feet and ran as fast as he could. He was off to a great start. Harriet fell behind, but she didn't want to lose. Harriet bounced as fast as she could and caught up to him!

"You are so pokey," she yelled.

Harriet ran past him. She was winning the race!

Herbert felt like hiding his head in his shell, but he kept running as fast as he could. After a few minutes, he spotted Harriet. She was sitting under a tree, nibbling a carrot.

As Herbert hurried by her, Harriet yelled, "You go ahead. I'll catch up after I finish my snack."

Herbert kept going. He could see the finish line. All his friends were waiting to see who would win. Herbert remembered all the things he had practiced and he sprinted for the line. He knew Harriet was close behind, but he went as fast as he could.

Herbert crossed the finish line first. "Herbert is the winner!" his friends yelled. "Hurray for Herbert!"

43

Name _____

Draw a picture of Herbert.

List two clues that told you about Herbert.

_____

_____

Draw a picture of Harriet.

List two clues that told you about Harriet.

_____

_____

Complete the following.

1. What is another name for this story?

_____

2. How do you think Herbert felt when his friends called him pokey?

_____

3. Why did Herbert feel like hiding his head in his shell?

_____

_____

4. How did Herbert's friends feel when he won the race?

_____

5. How do you think Harriet felt when Herbert won the race?

_____

What Will Happen?

Read each story. Circle the sentence that tells what will happen next.

• •

1. Autumn is almost over. Winter is on its way. It is getting cold. Soon, it will snow. The ducks take off.

    a. They go to eat.

    b. They fly south.

    c. They make nests.

2. The bird laid an egg. She sat on it for a long time. The egg began to crack.

    a. The bird flew away.

    b. The bird made a nest.

    c. A baby bird hatched.

Answer Key

Page 4
Cut/Paste: sand castle; beach ball; sailboat; fish

Page 5
Circle—Giraffe, rocket ship, tractor, turkey, moon, sled; 1. Answers will vary (Example: giraffe). 2. Answers will vary (Example: it belongs in the wild).

Page 6
Circle: A, B, C, E, F, H, I, J. Draw lines: A to bulletin girl; B to girl at desk with lined paper; C to boy at chalk board; E to boy with pencil; F to girl with paintbrush; H to girl holding hands up; I to girl with computer mouse; J to boy with paper

Page 7
A: fire station; B: fountain; C: hot dog stand; D: school; E: post office; F: toy store; G: grocery store; 1. Answers will vary.

Page 8
Circle: giraffe, dinosaur, post office, tall brick building; Color: chickens, pigs, horses. 1. rhino; 2. in the wild; Answers will vary.

Page 9
Order: Leon got a new bike. He rode his bike to the park. He rode back home. He put his new bike away.

Page 10
1. sled; 2. beach ball; 3. rattle; 4. jump rope; 5. doctor's bag; 6. basketball; 7. beach ball; He is wearing a swim suit. 8. doctor's bag; She is playing doctor.

Page 11
1. B; 2. C; 3. E. Circle: cookie cutter, bag of dog food, seed packet

Page 12
Order: 2, 1, 3. 1. Answers will vary.

Page 13
1. Answers will vary. 2. Answers will vary.

Page 14
Order: 6, 1, 5, 4, 3, 2

Page 15
1. bat; 2. chickens; 3. coat; 4. clown; 5. nap

Page 16
1. park; 2. school; 3. farm; 4. store

Page 17
1. B; 2. A; 3. D; 4. E; 5. C

Page 18
A. 3; B. 5; C. 6; D. 4; E. 1; F. 2

Page 19
1. carrot; 2. apple; 3. potato; 4. peach; 5. corn

Inferring • CD-104553

Page 20

1. yes; 2. yes; 3. no; 4. no; 5. no; 6. no

Page 21

1. a bike; Answers will vary (example: pumping). 2. baseball; Answers will vary (example: ball and bat).

Page 22

1. No, he has a barn. 2. Take them with him; he packs them up. 3. Yes, leaving makes him sad.

Page 23

Order: girl sleeping, sun rising, girl eating, girl on bus. 1. Answers will vary.

Page 24

1. squirrel; Answers will vary. 2. saving food; Answers will vary. 3. autumn; leaves on ground.

Page 25

1. Turtle; first clue; 2. A dog; first two clues

Page 26

1. B; 2. A; 3. A

Page 27

1. B; 2. C; 3. D; 4. E; 5. A

Page 28

1. bird; 2. fish; 3. spider; 4. lizard; 5. snake

Page 29

1. sisters; Answers will vary.
2. angry; 3. happy; 4. a dog;
5. Answers will vary.

Page 30

1. lizard; 2. picture of a lizard;
3. Answers will vary.

Pages 31–32

1. Answers will vary. 2. yard sales; answers will vary. 3. messy; Answers will vary. 4. money

Page 33

1. B; 2. C

Page 34

1. bath; 2. dog; 3. Answers will vary.
4. dry off; 5. He didn't want a bath.

Page 35

1. grocery store; 2. bag of food;
3. Isabella's brother; 4. Answers will vary. 5. Answers will vary. 6. Answers will vary.

Page 36

1. Tim's; 2. a bouquet; 3. a salad;
4. Tim's; 5. Circle: A, D, E

Page 37

1. excited; 2. worried; 3. good day

Page 38

1. which way to walk from the school
2. No; there is no church. 3. Go around the corner; 4. the house number

Page 39

1. rabbit; Answers will vary. 2. Math; added numbers. 3. Sammy ate it; Answers will vary. 4. Answers will vary.

Page 40

1. It snowed. 2. snow day; 3. sled
4. happy

Page 41

1. nice; 2. under; 3. pain; 4. big; 5. ruin

Page 42

1. tall; 2. big tantrum; 3. sad

Pages 43–44

Herbert is a turtle or tortoise. Answers will vary. 1. Tortoise and Hare; 2. sad; hurt; 3. He was sad. 4. happy; 5. sad

Page 45

1. B; 2. C

Inferring • CD-104553